Dedi

To my wonderful family and friends who are always there to brighten the day and provide love and support.

Copyright © Cheryl Lee-White 2020

Cheryl Lee-White has asserted her right to be identified as the author of this Work in accordance with the Copyright, Designs and Patents Act 1988.

All rights reserved.

No part of this publication may be reproduced, stored in a retrieval system, or transmitted in any form or by any means, electronic, mechanical, photocopying, recording or otherwise, without the prior permission of the copyright owner.

www.cherylleewhite.co.uk

A catalogue for this book is available from the British Library

Empowering Poetry

Believe

Cheryl Lee-White

Contents

Believe in You	1
Intuition	2
Dance to Your Own Beat	3
The Mountain is Calling	4
Prove Them Wrong	5
Breathe	7
You Matter	8
The Voice Inside Your Head	9
Beautiful and Unique	11
Set Yourself Time	12
Be Kind to Yourself	13
One Life	14
Courage	15
Get Stuck In	16
Be Thankful	17
Never Let Go of Your Dreams	18
Anxiety	19

You Have the Power	21
Love Yourself	22
Fear	23
Self-Worth	24
What if I Fail	25
24 Hours	26
Don't Let Life Pass You By	27
Self-Love	28
Be Mindful	29
Be a Butterfly	31
Let Joy Flood Your Soul	32
Wishing on a Dream	33
Progression	34
Bath Yourself in the Ocean	35
Be Grateful	36
Rainbow	37
Perfect in Your Own Way	38

Drown Out the Sound	39
Begin	40
Visualise Your Goal	41
Discipline	42
Slow Progress	43
Rise-Up	44
Don't Put Things Off	45
Flowers Bloom	46
Let Your Pain Be Felt	47
Scars	48
Attitude	49
Rock Bottom	50
Make Plans	51
Commit to Learning	52
Your Circumstances Don't Define You	53
Consistency	55
Pave Your Own Way	56

Better Than Yourself	57
Only the Destination	58
Your Rescue	59
Stars Shine in the Dark	60
Nature Be Your Healer	61
Give to Others	62
Comfort Zone	63
Winter	64
Consistency Not Perfection	65
Other Books By the Author	66
About the Author	67
Thank you	68

Believe in You

All your dreams can come true,

You just need to believe in you.

Intuition

Follow your intuition it knows what to do,

It is your inner compass that will guide you.

If in your intuition you trust and believe,

Then good things you will start to receive.

Dance to Your Own Beat

Dance to the beat of your own drum,

Don't feel the need to be like anyone.

Standout and be unapologetically you.

You don't have to follow what others do.

Be the wolf in a sea of sheep,

Dare to be different and unique.

Be true to who you really are,

And in life, you will go far.

The Mountain is Calling

The mountain is calling

So why are you stalling?

The trail may be rough

And the climb will be tough.

But the mountain will reward

Of this, you can be assured.

Prove them Wrong

'You should give up on that idea,

It is not going to work, I fear.'

Prove them wrong

'You don't have what it takes

To raise such high stakes.'

Prove them wrong

'You shouldn't get that degree,

Waste of time if you ask me.'

Prove them wrong

'You want to be an entrepreneur,

The challenges you'll never endure.'

Prove them wrong

'You want to be a millionaire

You're never going to make it there.'

Prove them wrong

Hold your head high and stay strong,
Do what you do and prove them wrong.

Breathe

Breathe,

Your head is filled with a million things to do,

And the overwhelm is consuming you.

Breathe,

Just take a minute and sit yourself down,

And think about what is making you frown.

Breathe,

Calm your mind, relax have a nice cuppa of tea,

With a clear head a way to solve your problems you'll see.

You Matter

When everything is going wrong,

And you are struggling to carry on,

I want you to know you matter.

When you are feeling the hurt and pain,

And try your hardest to stay sane.

I want you to know you matter.

When you feel you've no one to care,

And you are falling into despair

I want you to know you matter.

The Voice Inside Your Head

I am the voice inside your head,

Filling your thoughts with dread.

I put you off doing anything new,

By telling you, you're not good enough to.

I spread your self-doubt and fear from within,

Making sure that you never get that win.

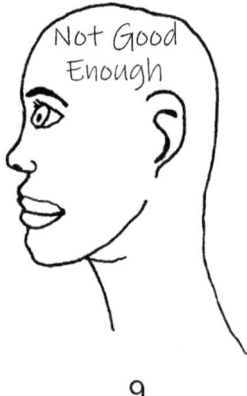

I am your heart and soul,

Helping you to get back in control.

I will help you get through,

When your inner voice is doubting you.

I know that you are strong and tough,

And you are more than enough.

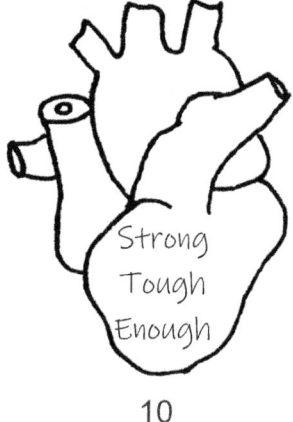

Beautiful and Unique

Our bodies are all unique,

With a diverse range of physiques.

All of them beautiful in their own way,

In an admirable contrasting display.

Know that you are beautiful just as you are,

And love every lump, bump and scar.

It doesn't matter if you are big, small, short or tall,

Everyone's body in its own way is beautiful.

Set Yourself Time

Set yourself time,

To relax and clear your mind.

Give meditation a go,

And get into the relaxing flow.

Meditation can take a while to feel at ease,

But with practice, it'll become a breeze.

So bask in the power of meditation,

And enjoy the feeling of relaxation.

Be Kind to Yourself

Could you ever imagine speaking to someone else,

The way you speak about yourself?

I don't think you would ever be so unkind.

So why to yourself do you leave kindness behind?

One Life

One life is all we get,

So don't fill it with regret.

Make every second count,

And those life experiences mount.

Grab every opportunity that comes your way,

As you never know when it will be your last day.

Courage

Courage isn't made overnight,

It comes from determination and fight.

It is the strength to persevere,

Despite the pain and fear.

Get Stuck In

Don't wait for the perfect moment to begin,

Get started now and get stuck in.

You'll pick it up and learn as you go,

And continue to develop and grow.

Be Thankful

Be thankful for every day,

And all the small things that come your way.

Be thankful for your health,

And fill your heart with gratitude and wealth.

Be thankful for the roof over your head,

And that you have a warm, comfy bed.

Be thankful for the knowledge you know,

And the learning you have left to grow.

Be thankful for nature all around,

And the soothing, calming sounds.

Be thankful for the air that you breathe,

And for every blessing you receive.

Never Let go of Your Dreams

Never let go of your dreams,

No matter how unattainable they seem.

As with hard work and dedication,

You'll be arriving at the dream station.

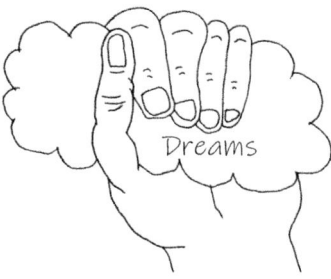

Anxiety

Your heart has started pumping,
You can feel your chest-thumping.

This anxiety is consuming you.

Your body is beginning to sweat,
As your mind starts to fret.

This anxiety is consuming you.

Your breathing is starting to accelerate,
And you can't seem to think straight.

This anxiety is consuming you.

The sick feeling within begins to rise,

As your stomach contents start to mobilise.

This anxiety is consuming you.

BREATHE!

Be still, let that anxiety ease.

Stay strong and you will get through.

And stop anxiety from consuming you.

You Have the Power

Today may have been a bad day,
Where nothing has gone your way,
It may have left you feeling down,
But you have the power to turn it around.

Take your focus off what went wrong,
Reset your thinking and move on.
Focus on the things that have gone right,
And ignite that positive thinking light.

Love Yourself

If you want love and respect

from someone else.

You first need to love

and respect yourself.

Fear

This fear has gripped you tight,

It's holding on with all its might.

The self-doubt is stopping you,

From doing what you want to do.

Just stop for a second and breathe,

Take deep breaths and let the tension ease.

Be still for a minute and let your mind clear,

In doing this your inner self you will hear.

Your inner self believes in you,

Knowing exactly what you can do.

It knows you can overcome this fear,

So have faith and trust in yourself, my dear.

Self-Worth

You are the only person

on this earth,

who gets to decide

your self-worth.

What if I Fail

What if I fail and fall,

And everything I do means nothing at all?

But what if you succeed and stand tall,

And in the end, achieve it all.

24 Hours

What are you going to do,

With the 24 hours that are given to you.

We all have the same amount every day,

But will you use them or idle them away.

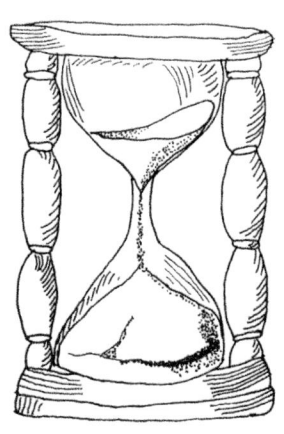

Don't Let Life Pass You By

Don't let life go by in a flash,

Slow down and stop the dash.

Take in all of your surrounds,

Listen out to all the sounds.

Notice the air, take a deep breath and inhale,

Look around you and take in every detail.

Self Love

To yourself nice things you need to say,

It may be the only nice thing you hear today.

So appreciate everything that you are and do,

And let that self-love grow inside of you.

By building your self-love and self-esteem,

It will let love and happiness inside you beam,

Having this wondrous self-love inside of you,

Will make you strong and less affected by what others do.

Be Mindful

Five senses we have been given,

Use them and be mindfulness driven.

See the birds in the trees,

See all the patterns in the leaves,

Be mindful.

Feel the air as it blows,

Feel the grass between your toes.

Be mindful.

Listen to the sounds that pass you by,

Listen to the sounds on the ground and in the sky.

Be mindful.

Smell the scents in the breeze,

Smell the scents that please.

Be mindful

Taste the veg that breaks the ground,

Taste the fruit juicy and round.

Be mindful.

Engage your senses in all that you do,

And let mindfulness immerse you.

Be a Butterfly

You can be that butterfly,

Soaring and flying high.

First, you need to be a caterpillar,

Heading into change that is unfamiliar.

Embrace change not knowing where it will lead,

As change has to come first before you succeed.

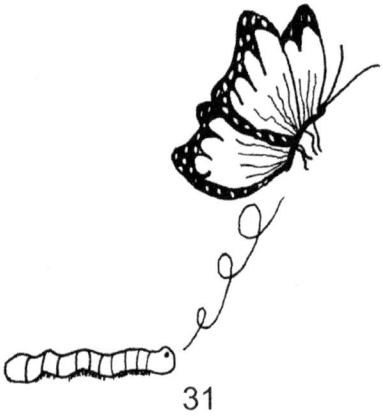

Let Joy Flood Your Soul

Find things daily to make you smile,

Let happiness sit with you for a while.

Allow the joy to flood into your soul,

Making your heart feel whole.

Wishing on a Dream

Wishing on a dream,

Doesn't make it come true,

it takes hard work and dedication

And that's down to you.

So roll up your sleeves,

And get stuck in.

Today is the day,

That you will begin.

It doesn't matter what you do,

it could just be one little thing.

But every task that you get done

Nearer to your dream it will bring.

Progression

Progression is progression,

No matter how small.

Any step forward,

Is better than none at all.

Bath Yourself in the Ocean

Bath yourself in the ocean of love,

Sent down to us from up above.

Wash away the pain and regret

And the fear of what hasn't happened yet.

Come out as pure and free,

And see the world as it be.

Be Grateful

Be grateful for the sun that brightens the day,

Be grateful for the moon which lights the way.

Be grateful for every breathe that you take.

Be grateful for every move that you make.

Rainbow

If you want to see a rainbow soar,

The storm you first have to endure.

Perfect in Your Own Way

To the mirror, the girl did say,

"I want to be perfect in every way."

The mirror replied, "How do you define perfection?

As perfection differs from every viewer's perception."

"Perfection comes from deep inside,

Where if you look you can decide,

To see perfection as how others say,

Or see that you're perfect in your own way."

Drown Out the Sound

You need to learn to drown out the sound,

When people try to put you down.

Your self-worth comes from you alone,

The only opinion that matters is your own.

Begin

Beginning can be scary,
And make you feel a little wary.

It can be a big step,
But there is no need to fret.

As beginning doesn't last long,
In no time you'll be sailing along.

Visualise Your Goal

If you can see yourself
achieving your goal,
And you believe it will happen
With your heart and soul.

Then you've already overcome
Your biggest obstacle,
And with some hard work,
The rest into place will fall.

Discipline

Discipline is at the centre of success

You need it or from your dreams, you'll digress.

Instil that discipline early on,

It will help when the motivation has gone.

Start to plant that discipline seed,

It is what you need to succeed.

Because if you can't win against yourself,

You won't win against anyone else.

Slow Progress

It doesn't matter how slow you go,

As long as there is progress to show.

Taking small steps every day,

Will ensure you head the right way.

Rise Up

Rise up above the haters.

Rise up above the naysayers.

Rise up from your mistakes,

No matter how long it takes.

Rise up from your downfalls.

Rise up high above them all.

Rise up to your higher self.

To happiness and wealth.

Don't Put Things Off

Don't put things off until tomorrow,

These will only cause you sorrow.

Take action and do them today

Don't let procrastination stand in your way.

Flowers bloom

A flower doesn't bloom for anyone else,

It will only bloom to please itself.

Let Your Pain Be Felt

Let your pain be felt,

Feel the heartache you were dealt.

Let it through your flow,

Until you are ready to let it go.

If you try to hide it away,

Your pain will forever stay.

Scars

Wear your scars with pride,

These are medals you shouldn't hide.

Each one a difficulty you have overcome,

Don't let embarrassment for them succumb.

Be proud of each and every scar,

They show just how strong you are.

Attitude

Your attitude is the difference
Between having a good day or bad.

Your attitude is the difference
If you feel happy or sad.

Your attitude is the difference
If you get angry or stay calm.

Your attitude is the difference
If you walk away or cause someone harm.

Don't fill your days full of strife
Change your attitude, change your life.

Rock Bottom

So you have hit rock bottom,

And you are feeling rotten.

You are not sure what to do,

And sadness is consuming you.

From the bottom, there is only one way to go.

It may be difficult and it may be slow.

But you will rise up and be stronger than before.

And then your happiness and success will soar.

Make Plans

Make plans for success.

Make plans to rest.

Make plans for activities.

Make plans for the possibilities.

Make plans to see friends.

Make plans to make amends.

Make plans for the ones you love.

Make plans to give you that shove.

Make plans but be sure to follow them through,

As endless opportunities are waiting for you.

Commit to Learning

Commit yourself to learning,

Keep your mind constantly turning.

Be a student in the university of life,

Where learning opportunities are rife.

Be open to the opportunities around you.

Always be prepared to learn something new.

Your mind will continue to develop and grow,

With each new piece of knowledge, you know.

Your Circumstances Don't Define You

It doesn't matter where you grew,

Or who in your family was there for you.

Your circumstances don't define you.

It doesn't matter if you've suffered in the past

Or if your marriage didn't last.

Your circumstances don't define you.

It doesn't matter if you've been abused.

Or in the past drugs, you have misused.

Your circumstances don't define you.

It doesn't matter if you suffer from depression

Or you lost everything in a recession.

Your circumstances don't define you.

Consistency

Discipline yourself to be consistent,

In this pursuit, you must be persistent.

With being constant comes great rewards,

So it is well worth working towards.

Constancy will help you develop faster,

And in your chosen field become a master.

It will build peoples trust and respect in you,

So make sure to be consistent in what you do.

Pave Your Own Way

Pave your own way,

Create your own path,

Don't listen to others,

If they say it's daft.

You may be the first,

To walk this way

But others will follow,

In your footsteps one day.

Be Better Than Yourself

Inspire yourself every day,

To be better than you were yesterday.

If every day you improve and grow

Imagine how much progress you'll show.

Only the Destination

Your dream is only the destination,
The journey takes hard work and dedication.

Your Rescue

No one is coming to your rescue,

It's sad but it's true.

People may help you along the way,

But it's up to you at the end of the day.

Stars Shine in the Dark

From the dark comes beauty.

A wonder for all to see.

Like the stars that twinkle in the night,

From the darkness, you can find your light.

Nature Be Your Healer

Let nature be your healer,

Let it be your spiritual dealer,

Let its power touch your soul

Making your mind and body whole.

Give to Others

Give to others with no thought of return,

In this service allow your heart to yearn.

Give without any expectations,

Make service part of your foundations.

Give to others without thought of reward,

And happiness in your heart will be stored.

Comfort Zone

If you leave your comfort zone behind,

You will surely begin to find,

That great things will start to come your way,

So get out of that comfort zone today.

Winter

Every year winter will appear,

And from it, you can not steer.

So prepare yourself for the cold days ahead,

And don't feel yourself with dread.

For the cold weather will not last,

And these dark times will pass.

With it, we will emerge in spring,

And ready for a new chapter to begin.

Consistently Not Perfection

It's got to be right,

And it's got to be good.

This is a concept,

That is so misunderstood.

Strive for consistency.

Not perfection.

Start with what you have

And improve with reflection.

Reviews

Thank you for purchasing and reading my book, it means a lot to me. If you have enjoyed my book, I would be extremely grateful if you could spare a few minutes to leave a review.

Other Poetry Books by the Author

Poetry to Inspire and Uplift is a collection of positive and uplifting poetry.

50% of all profits from 'Poetry to Inspire and Uplift' will be donated to Samaritans a registered charity.

About the Author

Cheryl Lee-White is an award-winning children's author and best selling poet who lives in Somerset, England, with her partner and 3 daughters.

Writing is her passion and she loves to share this with others through the joy of books.

Where to Find the Author

You can find the author at the following places -

www.cherylleewhite.co.uk - you can also subscribe to the newsletter to be kept up to date with new releases and blog posts.

www.facebook.com/cherylleewhiteauthor

www.instagram.com/cherylleewhiteauthor

Thank You!

Printed in Great Britain
by Amazon